LIGHT BEYOND THE SHADOWS

A TRUE STORY

SANGITA RAJE

Clever Fox®
PUBLISHING

CLEVER FOX PUBLISHING
Chennai, India

Published by CLEVER FOX PUBLISHING 2025

ISBN: 978-93-7500-170-6

In loving memory

Of

Two of the strongest women I knew

A piece of my soul, my mom

Usha Uday Kale

And

Three time undefeated cancer warrior, my mom-in-law

Usha Ramesh Raje

CONTENTS

PROLOGUE

Every life carries a story. Some stories begin quietly, slipping into the world without much notice. Others arrive with resistance, testing fate from the very first breath.

Mine belonged to the second kind.

Looking back, I realize that survival has been the recurring theme of my journey. Life has tested me again and again — through loss, through pain, through the unexpected twists that no one prepares you for. Yet at every turn, something — call it grace, destiny, or sheer stubborn will — has carried me forward.

This book is not just about my story, but about what life teaches when it pushes us to the edge and then pulls us back. It is about the invisible hands that hold us when all seems lost, and about the spirit that refuses to give up.

If you've ever wondered why you are here or doubted whether you have the strength to face what lies ahead, perhaps my story will remind you of a simple truth: **we are not here by accident. Life insists on us.**

And my battle began even before I opened my eyes.

CHAPTER 1

1963, MUMBAI — BATTLE FOR BIRTH

Having two babies within two years, my mother was completely unprepared to bring a third child — me — into this world. On the advice of a well-meaning friend, she took medication to terminate the pregnancy.

But I had other plans.

I refused to be eliminated.

Soon after, my mother fell very ill. When my father discovered what had happened, all hell broke loose. She was hospitalized, received medical care for several days, and was confined to bed rest for months. But eventually, I made it.

Then again, how could I arrive without a little drama?

I took my own sweet time. (Probably my way of exacting a bit of revenge — ha-ha!) And finally, one early morning, before the doctor could even reach the delivery room, I decided to make my grand entrance.

Panic struck as they discovered three cords wrapped tightly around my neck. A call went out for the doctor, but before she could arrive, an experienced midwife acted quickly.

Using both her thumbs, she gently slipped the cords over my head, saving my life.

Remember, this was a time when medical science hadn't advanced the way it has today. There were no sonographies, no specialized prenatal care — just instincts, experience, and courage. Yet battles were won in those days too.

And so, on a beautiful rainy morning — June 25th, 1963 — I was born. All nine and a half pounds of me. Fair-skinned, with springy, curly, reddish-golden hair (which later parted ways with me when my head was tonsured — a typical Indian tradition). I carried a reddish birthmark between my eyebrows, which still makes an occasional reappearance.

The doctor proudly displayed me as the *Amba Mata* of the hospital. After all, she had saved me from "demolition!" 😊

The Inspection

When my father arrived at the hospital, he was tied up in knots of worry. Without so much as a greeting to my mother, he asked the nurse to uncover me.

He conducted a meticulous inspection — finger by finger, toe by toe, arms, legs — making sure I had no deformities. He was terrified that the medicine my mother had taken might have left its mark on me. Only after confirming that I was normal and healthy did he finally speak to her.

On the second day, a nurse brought a baby from the nursery for feeding. One glance, and my mother knew something was wrong.

"This is not my baby," she cried. "My baby is very fair and has curly hair."

An alarm was raised. A frantic search began. After nearly two hours — and my mother's endless tears — they found me. In the general ward. Being happily breastfed by a '*doodhwali* '— a woman who milked cows for a living — who had delivered her own child two days earlier.

To this day, no one knows why she didn't realize the baby she was nursing wasn't hers. I'm told my mother's gynaecologist gave her a proper scolding — maybe even a slap. Thankfully, I was reunited with my relieved and exhausted mother.

First Lesson

Perhaps life had already whispered its first lesson to me that day — that existence is never guaranteed, it must be fought for.

From the very beginning, I learned that survival is not just a matter of chance, but of will, grace, and the mysterious hands that protect us when all seems lost.

My journey began not in certainty, but in defiance of endings — a reminder that every life is a miracle, claimed against impossible odds. Maybe that is why, even today, I believe we are not here by accident. We are here because Life itself insists on us.

Life tested me before I had even opened my eyes — perhaps to remind me that every birth is not just a beginning, but a victory of spirit over circumstance.

Ironically, my siblings always grumbled that Mom loved me the most.

And maybe… she did!

CHAPTER 2

1969, MUMBAI — THE COKE STORY

"Hurry up, we're getting late!" said my Aunt Witty. (She truly lived up to her nickname — her sense of humour was unmatched!)

We squeezed into Dad's red Herald — his favourite possession.

It was summer vacation, and we were headed to Juhu beach. Ours was a big, boisterous family. Dad had twelve siblings — six brothers and six sisters. A solid testament to how much my grandparents loved each other! We were a gang of twenty-four first cousins!

Being the eldest of the lot, Dad often hosted his sisters and their kids during the holidays.

We packed ourselves into five or six cars

and zoomed off — without Mom. Yes, you read that right — they forgot Mom!

Turns out, she was still in the kitchen, organising dinner for everyone. And in all the excitement, they left her behind — in the kitchen! We turned back, of course, to pick her up. But that day went down in family history. Dad was not allowed to forget it in a hurry!

Family outings to the beach were always a riot, and this one was no different. Uncles frolicked in the sea in their swimming trunks, and aunts waded in wearing saris.

Mom, as always, stood guard on the shore, watching us like a hawk. She was forever worried Dad would take us too far into the water and we'd drown. Every few minutes, she'd shout to bring us back closer to shore.

After all the fun in the sea and sand, we were starving. The aroma from the food stalls was irresistible — pani puri (crispy balls with spicy, tangy fillings), crispy dosas, and colourful golas (ice popsicles) — we devoured it all.

On our way back, my eight-year-old cousin and I — just nine months older than her — desperately needed to pee. We were riding in Aunt Witty's open-top car (a treat in itself!).

We stopped near a small, dingy restaurant, and my aunt asked us to go in and request permission to use the washroom. We walked into the restaurant. A dark, grumpy guy was sitting behind the restaurant counter. We asked him politely to allow us to use the washroom, but he refused,

saying we could only use the washroom if we bought something. We had no money on us and returned to the car, disappointed.

When my aunt asked what happened, we told her. Without a word, she got down and asked us to follow her. She walked into the restaurant and politely requested again to allow us kids to use the washroom. The manager refused again.

With a completely straight face, she said, "Okay, give me a Coke."

She paid for it, and we ran to use the washroom. When we returned, the Coke — a classic glass bottle — was still unopened on the counter.

Then came the twist.

My aunt calmly said to the manager, "Open the bottle." The manager did.

She looked him straight in the eye and asked him to open the refrigeration box. He hesitated but complied.

We watched, not knowing what she would do next.

And then — with zero expression, she poured the entire bottle of Coke into the refrigeration box.

Not a word. Not a pause. Just poured it all in.

He stood there stunned — maybe something about her face made him think twice about reacting.

She then turned, held our hands, and walked right out of the restaurant.

I was speechless. I still am, every time I recall that moment.

It's an incident I can never forget. No exchange of words. No display of anger. Never had I seen my ever-happy and smiling aunt have a deadpan look.

Yes, actions do speak louder than words.

That day, I learned something lasting — that dignity doesn't need a raised voice, and courage doesn't always wear a sword.

Sometimes, it's found in a calm face, a quiet gesture, and a bottle of Coke poured without a word.

True strength isn't loud — it's composed.

And sometimes, the most powerful protest is the one that leaves others speechless — not with anger, but with grace.

CHAPTER 3

1970, MUMBAI — FIRST BRUSH WITH SPIRITUALITY

My grandfather was a man of remarkable contrasts. On one hand, he held high positions — Collector of Baroda, ADC to Late Shri Sayaji Rao Gaikwad — and played a role in India's agricultural progress by introducing the soybean plant from China, presenting it personally to the then Prime Minister Nehru. On the other hand, he chose to step away from privilege, moving to Mumbai with his twelve children and embracing an austere life. Whether that was a good decision for his children is debatable.

He was deeply spiritual, well-read, and disciplined. He gave up non-vegetarian food entirely and devoted long hours each day to meditation.

One evening, when I was about seven or eight years of age, his meditation went on for an unusually long time. The sun had dipped low, yet he remained seated in silence before a picture of Shri Ramakrishna Paramahansa. My grandmother grew anxious. She and others called his name softly, but he gave no response.

No one dared shake him; they feared that bringing him out of a deep trance suddenly could harm him. A lot of time had passed. They had been unsuccessful in bringing him back.

My grandmother started crying softly. A call was made to someone with spiritual knowledge. She suggested a strong-smelling flower should be held under his nose. Finally, a strong-scented flower was procured and held under his nose.

I remember watching in amazement as he slowly stirred, tears flowing down his cheeks. He shook his head gently, as if saying, *"No, don't bring me back."* That moment became etched in my young mind, a glimpse of a spiritual depth I could barely comprehend.

After that, he began meditating at a nearby Jain temple, seeking solitude. Sometimes I would quietly follow him, hoping to find where he sat. I never did. Instead, I found myself absorbed in the temple's calm, enjoying the quiet presence of that sacred space.

Back at home, my grandmother's pujas became my anchor. I would wake at four in the morning, join her in gathering flowers (often mischievously plucked from neighbours' gardens). Those mornings often ended with oranges in the garden and a game of badminton, simple joys wrapped in the fragrance of devotion.

When back home, I would sit beside her as she performed her puja, offering the flowers we gathered and reciting shlokas.

It was a passing phase, perhaps, but it was also the first doorway to my spiritual journey. Fragile, fleeting, yet profound, it planted in me a seed that never fully disappeared.

CHAPTER 4

1973, MUMBAI — TELEPATHIC VISION

We were three siblings, and my mother always wanted the best education for us. My sister and brother were sent to respective hostels in Pune, while I, being the youngest, was admitted to a reputed school downtown. Since it was far from our home in the suburbs, I was sent to live with my maternal grandmother, who lived close to the school.

The school was good, and I attended for a few days. But one afternoon, while lying next to my grandmother, I suddenly said, "Ba, I can see two fans." Horrified, she pointed at various objects around the room, asking how many of each I could see. To her dismay, I kept replying, "Two!" (Hahaha!) Without a second thought, she hired a taxi and rushed me back home. And just like that, my brief stint at that school near my grandmother's place ended.

After much effort, my parents got me into a day-boarding school with a sprawling campus. Students ate lunch there, played games and did self-study. They were sent home by evening. On the very first day, dressed neatly and full of excitement, I walked in happily—until I saw the nuns. Dressed in brown and black habits, with large beads hanging around their necks, they looked intimidating. Something about those beads terrified me. I cried, clung, and fought so fiercely that they had no choice but to take me back home. My poor mother's dream of putting me in a prestigious school was shattered yet again.

Finally, I was admitted to a convent school in our suburb, where I went on to study for the next few years.

I was a good student but painfully shy, hardly ever speaking in class.

Our school arranged outstation trips every year, but I seldom joined—until seventh grade, when my parents decided it was time. A small lavender suitcase was bought, new clothes packed, and I was sent off, nervous yet excited.

The trip was wonderful. We visited Bangalore, Ooty, and Mysore. I remember eucalyptus-scented forests, laughing, enjoying with new friends, and buying Mysore sandalwood soaps for my mother and family. To everyone's surprise—including my own—I didn't miss my mother during the entire trip, even though I was away from her for the first time.

This was unusual for me, because throughout my childhood, I was inseparable from her. I was fiercely possessive, almost jealous of anyone to whom she paid attention. If an older cousin wore her saree (which they often did!) I would point a remark loudly, "That's my mom's saree!" earning laughter and teasing for being so possessive.

But as the train rolled back toward Mumbai, something shifted. A wave of longing for my mother hit me, and I grew tearful. Strangely, I began seeing her in my mind's eye—different from her usual self. I pictured her in a yellow saree, oiled hair, pulled back and tied in a bun, a large vermilion dot on her forehead, her big eyes filled with worry.

The vermilion dot was a constant, but the oiled, tied-back hair was not like her at all. The image kept flashing before me, along with an ache in my heart.

When the train reached Dadar station, most children were picked up by waiting parents. But no one came for me. Slowly, the crowd thinned until only I was left with a school staff member who kindly waited beside me. Those were days without mobile phones—there was no way to check what had happened.

And then, I saw her. My mother hurried towards me, wearing a yellow saree, with her hair oiled and tied back into a bun, a big vermilion dot glowing on her forehead, and her eyes wide with worry. Exactly as I had envisioned her.

Later, I learned she had completely forgotten my return date. At the last minute, she tried to arrange for someone closer to Dadar station to pick me up, since we lived in Chembur, which was a good half an hour away. When that didn't work out, she panicked, tied back her oiled hair without bathing, and rushed straight to the station.

To this day, I wonder—how did I see her that way, before she even arrived? Was it her worry that reached me? Was it my longing that summoned her image? Did our souls meet halfway in that moment? I'll never know.

It was the first and the last time I had such a vivid vision. Intuition has often guided me since, but never again a vision like that.

CHAPTER 5

1969, PUNE — WHEN GOD WALKED WITH ME

I was about six years old. Both my elder siblings were studying in a hostel in Pune. Every weekend, my parents would drive down from Mumbai to visit them, and I always tagged along. We had a routine — we'd stay in the same hotel every time. It felt familiar, almost like our weekend home.

One such afternoon, around lunchtime, we had just arrived and were settling into our hotel room. Mom and Dad were inside, deciding what to order for lunch. The hotel boy stood just outside the door, waiting for our order.

I stood at the door, with my little hands on the frame, swinging my legs playfully in and out of the room. It was a windy day — the kind of wind that whispers secrets through the trees and pushes clouds around like toys in the sky.

Then came a sudden, strong gust. Before anyone could react, the wind slammed the heavy hotel door shut.

Mom and dad were inside.

I was outside.

My two tiny middle fingers were stuck inside the door hinge.

The door had crushed them.

I let out a piercing scream.

What followed was nightmarish...

My father heard my scream and stood frozen in fear. He was in a state of shock—unable to move, unable to process what was happening. I kept screaming, "Open the door!" It felt like ages before he finally did.

As the door opened, my fingers were released. I stood there, staring blankly—not at my hand, but at my parents' horrified faces. They were staring at my fingers, and I was staring at them. There was no pain. Just numbness.

Then, instinctively, I looked down at my hand. And let out a blood-curdling scream. My fingers were a dangling mess, barely hanging by shreds of skin—twisted, limp, almost unrecognizable.

My mother, stunned and disoriented, ran down the stairs in a panic. She cried out to every passerby, "Did you see what happened to my daughter?" Her voice was shrill, wild with disbelief and helplessness. She reached the hotel lobby, and the manager, realizing she was not in her senses, threw a jug of water on her face.

Trying to calm her, he quickly brought her back upstairs in the elevator. Meanwhile, my father gently wrapped his handkerchief around my mangled fingers, hoping to give them some support.

Surprisingly, there wasn't much bleeding. The pain hadn't hit me yet. There was only a dull throbbing. It was like a heart was thumping inside my fingers.

The manager suggested a good orthopaedic surgeon, and Daddy drove us straight to the hospital. All through the ride, Mom kept asking me to chant "Om Namah Shivaya," and that's exactly what we did — just the two of us, crying and repeating it together like a prayer thread tying us to hope.

When we reached the hospital, we were told that both the surgeon and the anaesthetist had just gotten into their car, about to leave for lunch. But then something miraculous happened. A junior doctor ran out and pleaded with them to come back and take a look at me. To this day, I believe God came in the form of that man — the one who kept requesting, insisting. Later, my father told us how he had heard the doctor pleading in Marathi:

"Phula sarkhi mulgi aahe"

("She's a flower-like child. Please come and see her.")

The surgeon did come back. One look at my fingers and he understood the gravity of the situation. He immediately ordered an X-ray. While I was still lying on the X-ray table, the surgeon walked in and began discussing the images with the radiologist. I didn't understand most of what they were saying — but thanks to all the Enid Blyton books I had devoured, I understood just enough English to grasp one terrifying truth: they were talking about amputating my fingers.

I broke down, crying harder than ever. Through my sobs, I kept pleading with the surgeon:

"Please, promise me you won't cut off my fingers."

Each time, he tried to pacify me.

"We won't."

But I wasn't convinced. My voice, trembling and insistent, rose again and again:

"Say God Promise."

Finally, the doctor turned to me, and with a quiet firmness said:

"God Promise."

And I was young enough to believe that no one could ever break a God Promise.

He then explained to my parents that he would attempt to reattach both fingers. But he also warned them — on the third day, they would remove the bandages. If there was no sign of blood circulation, another operation would be needed. Amputation would then be inevitable.

Another blessing: I had an empty stomach, which meant they could take me into surgery immediately. Anaesthesia can't be given on a full stomach — and this little detail, too, felt like the universe had prepared me for that moment.

Back then, reattaching severed body parts was extremely rare. The first limb reattachment surgery had just taken place in May 1962 in Boston, USA, by Dr. Ronald Malt. Yet, this surgeon chose to try.

And for that, I will forever be grateful.

CHAPTER 6

1969, PUNE — THE LETTER OF THANKS

I remember waking up to a throbbing pain in my fingers. It was unbearable. The room was dark, and I began to cry softly. Only the nightlight cast a faint glow across the room. A moment later, the lights came on. My maternal grandmother, my mother, and my father were all by my side, trying their best to comfort me. To distract me from the pain, someone was always there—playing board games, telling stories, just being present.

On the third day, I was taken back to the hospital. The doctors needed to check if blood circulation had returned to my severed fingers. I wasn't allowed to have my parents with me. The nurses positioned themselves in such a way that I couldn't see my operated hand. (I don't remember seeing my fingers properly until much later—after my plastic surgery.)

A while later, my mom and dad were called into the room. The surgeon, smiling, announced that my fingers had regained blood circulation. They wouldn't need to be amputated after all.

Months later, after a successful plastic surgery in Mumbai, my plastic surgeon gave my mom a letter to deliver personally to my surgeon in Pune. He said, "Please hand this to him the next time you visit."

A few weeks later, we were back in Pune for the weekend. Mom and Dad had gone to visit my sister at her hostel, so I went with my maternal grandmother to meet the surgeon who had saved my fingers. We carried a box of sweets as a small token of our gratitude, along with the letter.

He read the letter aloud in front of us. One line stayed with me forever:

"After seeing the X-ray, I have to commend you for trying to save these fingers. I wouldn't have even attempted it."

Then the surgeon looked at my grandmother and said, "I tried because I thought—if that little child has so much faith in her God, why shouldn't I give it a chance?"

"Years later, I look at my fingers and see two faint marks—just tiny dots left behind as reminders of that day. To anyone else, they are just scars. But to me, they are proof of faith, of miracles, and of a surgeon who chose to try."

CHAPTER 7

1970, MUMBAI — THE FLIRTY CAR

No television. No mobiles. No social media. Yet, life felt like a picnic.

Books were my solace. Football was my brother's. (He was brought back from the hostel as he kept falling sick too often.)

Our weekly outings—to the beach or a downtown restaurant—were the biggest highlights.

Traffic in those days was nothing like it is today. Roads were often empty, almost meditative in their stillness.

I still remember Mom complaining to Dad, "Why does the car always veer toward any pretty girl standing at a crossing?"

Dad would laugh mischievously and say, "Hey! It's not me—it's the car!"

Every time a young girl walked on the roadside, he would let go of the steering just a little and say with mock surprise,

"See? The car is the culprit—it's heading toward her all by itself!"

And true to his words, the car would gently drift—left or right—towards wherever the 'pretty young thing' happened to be.

I secretly believed Dad's car shared his flirtatious heart! Another time we were returning late from a trip to the Gateway of India and dinner at my father's favourite restaurant, 'Khyber.' In those days, good restaurants were uncommon. This was one of Dad's regular restaurants in Mumbai or as we knew it back then, 'Bombay.' They served very tasty chutney pomfret in those days which we all enjoyed eating very much. In fact, my mom was once allowed in the kitchen by the chef to see how it was prepared. She learnt it from that gracious chef and I learnt to cook it from her.

Our dinner at Khyber was followed by a late-night movie. On our way back, the roads were practically empty. (And my father was always a cautious driver. I think 40 or max 50 speed.) Out of the blue, a car sped past us unnecessarily too close. Dad saw it was a Sardarji and called out, "Sardarji kya baat hai? The Sardarji just put out his hand and indicated his watch. My dad checked his watch and saw it was 12 O'clock. Instead of getting mad at the Sardarji driver, we all burst out laughing. In those days, Sardarji's 12 o'clock jokes were so popular and loved by all.

The ability of a person to accept his mistake and make light of things is so rare. Till date, I remember that stranger with the ability to laugh at himself.

The Day My Father Fed a Dream

My dad was also a regular patron at "*Fredericks*", one of the first few authentic Chinese restaurants in Bombay back then. We'd often drive down for dinner, and much to his annoyance, we kids always fussed. (I'd stick to just soup and dessert, and my brother could be found sitting under the table sullenly 😄) But, with a lot of coaxing, we tasted and maybe started appreciating Chinese cuisine a little bit, over a period of time.

One evening, as we settled in, a commotion broke out near the entrance. A poorly dressed man was trying to enter the restaurant. The staff were stopping him, refusing him entry. He kept insisting he had the money to pay and showed them a small cloth bag filled with coins and a few crumpled notes.

Sensing the situation, my father stepped in. Calmly, he spoke to the manager, asking him to let the man in and assuring him that he would personally take care of the bill. Having known my father as a long-time customer, the manager hesitantly agreed.

The man—who turned out to be almost blind—was seated at a quiet corner. My dad told the waiter, *"Let him eat whatever he wants."*

My father asked the waiter to serve him whatever he wished to eat. And eat he did—with joy and gratitude written all over his face.

Before leaving, he requested to be taken to the person who had paid for his meal. When he was brought to our table, he folded his hands, then suddenly dropped to my father's feet in gratitude. He said he had been begging on the streets outside that restaurant for years. It had been his dream to one day eat at "*Fredericks*". He had saved for years to make that dream a reality.

That night, my father didn't just pay for a meal. He fulfilled a dream, gave dignity to a man who had almost been turned away, and quietly reminded me—once again—what true generosity looks like.

CHAPTER 8

1974, MUMBAI — MAN WITH THE MIDAS TOUCH

Life was blissful while Dad walked this earth. We lost him to lymph cancer when I was just eleven, my brother twelve and a half, and my sister thirteen and a half.

He was a self-made man—successful, dignified, and full of warmth. He started his career as a branch manager at a fire extinguisher company and went on to become a thriving entrepreneur. A man with a striking personality and an even larger heart, he carried responsibilities far beyond his own family.

He was always ready to help others. Whenever Mom expressed concern that he wasn't saving enough for us, he would chuckle and say, "I'm your blank cheque—don't worry, you can always encash me." And he believed it. I've seen him quietly buy groceries for relatives in need, pay for another's child's dance class, and even part with Mom's jewellery to help someone's daughter get married. He was a family bank.

To this day, I have never met a more giving soul.

Once, on his way to work, he noticed a crowd gathered on a street in Mumbai, causing a traffic jam. Curious, he stopped to ask a bystander what had happened. To his horror, he learned that a poor labour-class woman had gone into labour right there on the pavement—and people were merely watching.

Without a moment's hesitation, Dad stepped out of the car, bought a roll of fabric from a nearby shop, and urged a few women from the crowd to help form a curtain around her for privacy. Thankfully, one of them—a social worker—came forward to assist. Right there, on the noisy, chaotic street, the woman gave birth with dignity, because one man chose to care..

That was my father. The man with the Midas touch—not turning things to gold, but transforming lives with love.

But life is unpredictable.

My father passed away suddenly at the age of 42, leaving our family's bank coffers empty. Overnight, our world turned upside down.

As if that loss wasn't enough, my grandfather passed away just two months later.

It was said that my grandfather willed himself to pass. He had announced to the family that he would be gone after three days. The doctors were baffled that his pulse was beating, but his heart had stopped beating. He took the path of 'icha mrityu'. It is believed that evolved beings with yogic power can choose their time to exit their body.

Grief seemed to come in waves. Soon after, my maternal grandmother also left us. She had always been close to my father; he was her favourite son-in-law, always teasing her, making her laugh. She saw in him the son she never had. Perhaps she could not bear to see her daughter widowed so early. She too had lost her husband at a young age and had raised two daughters on her own. Watching her beloved daughter become a widow at just thirty-four years of age, shattered her heart. And maybe, in some ways, she gave up too.

All the losses within a span of one year brought us three siblings closer to each other. We became each other's strength. My sister too had been brought back from Pune due to some health issues when in the 9th grade. She had left the hostel just one year before dad passed.

That year took away so much—our father, our grandfather, our maternal grandmother. But it also gave us the unshakable bond of togetherness. From then on, we were not just siblings, we were each other's shelter.

Life had tested us with loss after loss, but perhaps that was its way of teaching us that while people leave, love never does. And love was the only inheritance our father left behind—the richest one of all.

CHAPTER 9

1973, MUMBAI — WHO IS THIS STRANGER?

Life was blissful as a child before Dad passed away— every festival was a celebration with a house full of music and laughter. Ours was a family of singers. My dad played the tabla, and two of my aunts sang like professionals — one could mimic Lata Mangeshkar effortlessly, the other was all about Asha Bhosale. Dad sang K. L. Saigal classics with heart, while my older uncle sang Talat Mahmood songs and the younger one belted out Kishore Kumar hits. Full-on entertainment, every single time.

Music was in the air — and in my soul. I had a small transistor that felt like my second skin.

My earliest memory of my sister is... almost odd. When she was suddenly pulled out of the hostel and brought home, it felt as if a stranger had walked into our house. Until then, we only saw her during quick weekend trips to Pune or during her short annual vacation. She had been in the hostel since I was a year old — from kindergarten all the way to ninth grade. And now, suddenly, she was here. In *our* home. With a big trunk. Fluent in English. Very pretty. And everyone was saying — "She's your sister."

I remember wondering — *Do I have to share my mom with her now?*

That's when it first sank in. This girl I had only seen occasionally was *my sister*, and she was going to live with us. I wasn't exactly thrilled at first. I didn't want to share my mother with anyone.

But time does its magic.

Having a sister who was so beautiful, so polished — it soon became a thrill. I was almost in awe of her. She was someone I *liked* to show off to my friends (not that I had too many). Her handwriting was like pearls. Slowly, we began to bond. But it was my brother and she who formed the real gang. Just the two of them. I often felt like an outsider.

She joined my school and quickly made many friends. It felt like she belonged to every place she stepped into.

I think she broke more than a few hearts when Mom married her off at just 16 years of age.

But she was happy.

I still remember her giving me a pearl ring she used to wear. "Don't worry," she said, "I'll support Mom however I can. You keep this ring. I'll keep giving you little things now and then."

Little did either of us know what life had in store for us.

CHAPTER 10

1974, MUMBAI — A LESSON LEARNT

Dad's passing brought with it many unspoken changes.

The milk tasted thinner — watered down, perhaps to stretch it a little longer. The bread barely held any butter. But even in that frugality, we stayed tightly knit.

My brother, who had always done everything but study, suddenly began taking life a bit more seriously.

After he was brought back from the hostel in Pune, our parents enrolled him in one of the most prestigious schools in Mumbai. It was a little far from where we lived, so a driver would drop him off and pick him up.

One day, my mother got a call from the school. "Your son hasn't been attending classes for quite some time now," they said.

To their horror, it was discovered that my brother had been getting off at the school gate every morning — only to head straight to a nearby garden. He'd spend his entire day there, eating his lunch under a tree and then returning home in the evening with the driver, right on schedule as if nothing was amiss.

Needless to say, he was promptly shifted to a school much closer to home — in fact, one right next to mine.

My brother had a big personality packed into a small body. He was popular, generous, and full of life. Believe it or not, he could drive a car at the age of nine or ten — without ever being taught! His tiny feet barely reached the brakes, but that never stopped him. Every time Dad felt sleepy while driving back from our evening outings, my brother would take over the steering wheel. Dad would doze off sitting on the driving seat, and my brother would creep in between the bucket seat of our Red Herald to control the steering and change gears if required. Lucky for us, the roads were practically empty in those days.

There was a gang of unruly boys from the nearby slum area who would cross our compound wall to reach the government school next door. They were loud, abusive, and often made everyone in our building uncomfortable with their catcalling and general misbehaviour.

My brother, just ten years old then, decided he had had enough. He took it upon himself to confront them. I don't know exactly what words were exchanged, but after that, the mischief stopped.

It was during Diwali, my brother told me, "Take the ladoos Mom made, but don't eat them. Give them to me. I'm collecting them for a secret reason."

I felt so important — part of a top-secret mission led by my hero brother.

Later, I found out he had gathered around 30-40 ladoos and handed them over to those very boys. He made a deal with them — if they behaved well for a week, there would be some tasty sweets coming their way. And it worked.

Despite his street-smart charm, studies and my brother never got along.

One incident I can never forget. This was before my father passed away. One day, I saw my mother silently crying while getting ready to go out. Her beautiful big eyes, usually full of life, were flowing with tears. I kept asking what was wrong, but she wouldn't answer.

Eventually, I found out that my brother had failed all his tests and had hidden the answer sheets under mom's bed. My mother had discovered them accidentally while cleaning. He had even gone so far as to forge her signature on the report card and taken someone else as his guardian to school when the teacher had called a meeting.

But what shocked me most wasn't his mischief — it was my mother's reaction. She didn't scold him. When he came back from his evening football game, she simply looked at him with tears streaming down her cheeks and said, "You lied to me?"

That one sentence carried so much pain — the fact that her son had lied to her, hurt her more than his failure ever could.

Unknowingly, in that moment, I learned a life lesson: Our lies can hurt more than our actions.

Strangely enough, after Dad passed away, the same boy who once ran away from books suddenly started passing all his exams. He never failed a single subject. He became very protective of us. He ensured we were happy. Every day he would sit at the lunch table and recount his day at school so hilariously and that it would make us laugh till tears rolled down our cheeks.

It was as if he had grown up overnight.

Maybe growing up isn't about age or exams.

Maybe it begins the moment you realise you've broken someone's trust — and promise yourself never to do it again.

Maybe it begins when your young shoulders first carry the weight of responsibility, when life silently whispers that you are now the man of the house.

CHAPTER 11

1977, GWALIOR — BALIKA BADHU

Some souls arrive like whispers of dawn, Not meant to linger, just to touch and be gone.

They light the sky, then fade from sight, Brief as a breeze, yet burning bright.

In moments fleeting, they leave their mark, A spark of love in places dark.

They teach us how to truly see— That even short lives can set us free.

They couldn't understand what went wrong.

"It's a brain infection," they said.

The best doctors attended to my adorable sister.

But sometimes, even medicine has no power against God's will.

We lost her.

But she left behind a precious part of her — a beautiful little angel. Her daughter.

About a year later, the whispers began.

"The child needs a mother who will love her like her own."

And there I was.

A balika badhu — a child bride.

All of fifteen. Married… and suddenly a mother.

Big shoes. Small feet.

It was a complete 360° shift.

To me, marriage had only meant new clothes and no school.

But when life gives you oranges… you make marmalade.

I adapted.

I embraced my new life. And, amidst a Tsunami of changes, I gave my board exams privately… and passed with flying colours!

The First Omelette

I still remember the first time my husband asked me to make an omelette.

I confidently walked into the kitchen… and then stood there, completely clueless.

It felt more complicated than a chemistry equation! 😄

After a few baffled moments, I sheepishly walked back out and asked him,

"Umm… how exactly do you make an omelette?"

He told me. I followed his instructions.

Whether it turned out edible — only he or God knows! 🙈 😂

But he ate it without a word, and I took that as a win. ♡

The age difference between me and my husband made it very difficult for me to fit into his world. I was a mere child in the midst of grown-ups.

At fifteen, I was suddenly "aunty" to many unmarried maidens who were older than me. Strangely enough, I took it in my stride.

My mother-in-law, sensing my loneliness, often took me to her kitty club meetings. Her friends were kind and indulgent, but they were all far older — older than even my mom. I smiled, I was respectful, but deep inside, I felt like a fish out of water.

My husband continued to socialise by himself. He would spend hours together with his friends at the local club, leaving me with long hours of solitude. The house was full of helpers. There were more of helpers than family members. My little daughter had both a day maid and a night maid, and naturally, she was more attached to them. To her, I was a new and unfamiliar figure.

So I turned to my true childhood companions — my books and my music. I slipped into the world of words and melodies, where I could still be a child, yet also dream of who I might become.

I was just a teenager, whom life had enrolled in an accelerated syllabus. And slowly, chapter by chapter, I began to grow into the role destiny had written for me.

CHAPTER 12

1979, GWALIOR — THE HARDEST GOODBYES

A few years after my marriage, Mom had to sell her flat in Mumbai and move to Gwalior. My brother too had to leave his prestigious college in Mumbai and join a college in Gwalior instead. At the time, it must have felt like a setback for them, but their move turned out to be a blessing in disguise — especially for a young bride like me, uprooted from her home and struggling to adjust.

I still remember how Mom, knowing my love for movies, would take an autorickshaw, come to pick me up, and take me to the cinema. I don't know if she could really afford those outings, but she never let it show. I would eagerly wait for those little escapes with her — moments of joy stitched into an otherwise difficult phase of my life.

My brother eventually completed his graduation, got married, and took up a job that posted him out of Gwalior. It broke my heart to watch him struggle, yet there was so little I could do to help.

By the time they moved out of Gwalior, I was in my twenties — a young woman ready to step into society with confidence. I not only learnt to host parties successfully, but also started many ladies' clubs that became quite popular. These clubs were more than just social gatherings; they gave me a sense of purpose, belonging, and the confidence that I could build something of my own. It was a socially engaging and fulfilling period of my life.

I made some very close friends, two of whom later shifted out of Gwalior. One of them was also my baby-bump friend — we both gave birth to sons just one day apart. Though she later relocated to a different city, we remained in close touch. A few years later, she fell ill. I visited her just before she passed away. That farewell remains the hardest goodbye of my life. I hugged her over and over again, unable to let go, until it was finally time to leave.

A few weeks later, I was sitting alone in my room. The house was quiet when I suddenly heard a swishing sound slip in through the gap in the door. I froze. A strange presence seemed to hover for a moment. The air felt heavy, yet oddly calm, and then, with the same swishing sound, the energy drifted out. I sat still, shaken and unsure of what I had just experienced.

An hour or so later, I received a call from her husband. My friend had passed away that very morning. Was that her? Had she come to see her son, who was then studying in a hostel in Gwalior? Had she stopped by to see me, too? Those questions will never have answers, but the moment remains etched in my heart.

A few years later, my brother moved to Canada, hoping for better prospects. Not long after, Mom too shifted there. It was yet another heart-wrenching goodbye. We drove down to Delhi to see her off. On our way, we stopped for a few hours in Agra.

My mom had always dreamt of visiting the Taj Mahal, and ironically, despite living just two hours away from Agra, in Gwalior, she had never seen it. When I asked my husband, he readily agreed to stop in Agra so she could finally witness the monument of love. Mom was overjoyed. We clicked pictures together and spent precious mother-and-daughter moments that I still treasure deeply.

My tears simply wouldn't stop after seeing her off at the airport.

The next morning, I was in shambles. Sensing my grief, my husband — knowing my love for movies — took me to a cinema. For those few hours, as I lost myself in the film, my tears would pause, only to return once a song sequence started or the lights came back on. That day, for the first and the last time in his life, my husband took me to two movies back to back. We stepped out of one show, bought tickets for another, and went in again. He was at a complete loss for how to pacify me. Somehow, that simple act of thoughtfulness helped take my mind off momentarily from the heaviness I felt in my heart.

Not being able to see Mom and my brother for years at a stretch was indescribably painful. Yet, I reminded myself that just as her move to Gwalior had once been a blessing in disguise for me, her move to Canada was a blessing for my brother's future — even if it left me with the ache of distance.

Sometimes, love also means letting go — allowing your loved ones to grow, even if it means accepting the loss that comes with their absence.

CHAPTER 13

1983, GWALIOR — GOD HEARD ME

I had happily settled into domestic life—busy hosting parties and enjoying a vibrant social circle. We had two maids to look after my daughter, and my mother-in-law was always at the helm when it came to managing her affairs.

I remember sitting in the sun on cold wintery afternoons and peeling fresh green pea pods. As I sat there, a baby goat (kid) came to the door, and I fed it the peels of the pea pods. Soon, it became a ritual. The goat belonged to a Muslim family, our neighbours and my husband's friend. Then came Eid. And with it came the delicious kebabs from our neighbours. How I loved those tasty kebabs! But after a few days I inquired about the goat and realised that I had eaten it...the kebabs! Didn't know whether to laugh or cry! I haven't eaten meat since then.

Four years into our marriage, I conceived. It was an extremely difficult pregnancy—bed rest, daily injections, weekly antibiotic shots, constant nausea, and severe allergic reactions. The entire gamut.

Finally, on a cold winter's day, my son was born—a healthy, fair bundle of joy. He was born a good 8 and a half pounds. Our family felt complete.

When he was around two years old, he began running a low-grade fever. It made him cranky and restless. We consulted a paediatrician, but he couldn't figure out the cause. The fever would come and go, every second day. Still no answers. We saw another paediatrician, but again—no diagnosis. My son also began to lose his appetite, which worried me even more. It had been nearly two months of this.

One evening, I asked my husband to take him for a drive—maybe a change of scene would cheer him up. We drove out of the city with our little boy nestled in my lap. It was a quiet drive. Neither of us spoke. We were both consumed with worry.

On our way, we crossed a small hill crowned by an Ancient Hindu Goddess temple. The stone steps of the temple began right at the foot of the hill, inviting every passerby upward. We drove past it without pause.

But on our return, I heard the bells inside the temple ringing, and something within me shifted. As we passed the temple again, I found myself silently praying — from the depths of my heart, with tears welling in my eyes. It was not an ordinary prayer; it was a mother's plea to the Mother of all:

"Please, Mata Rani… heal my son. I cannot bear to see him suffer. Give me his suffering instead."

Breaking the silence, I shared with my husband what I had just prayed. He remained quiet. We reached home, still wrapped in silence.

But, believe it or not, just a few days later, my son began to recover. He was cheerful again, his fever gone. And then… I began running a low-grade fever. The same kind, low grade fever that had afflicted him. It stayed with me for two whole years.

Coincidence? Maybe. But I like to believe that God had heard me.

Mata Rani had answered my prayers.

She had healed my son. 🙏

CHAPTER 14

1985, GWALIOR — WHEN GOD SPEAKS THROUGH A FRIEND

"Your ears shall hear a word behind you, saying, 'This is the way, walk in it,' when you turn to the right or when you turn to the left."

– Isaiah 30:21

The fever continued. I would often get allergies and have a lot of joint pain.

On the advice of doctors in Gwalior, we travelled to Mumbai, as the tests I needed weren't available locally at the time.

A well-known senior doctor was consulted in Mumbai. After a series of tests, I was diagnosed with an autoimmune disease — *Systemic Lupus Erythematosus* (SLE). Autoimmune conditions occur when the immune system mistakenly attacks the body's own healthy cells.

I was advised to strictly avoid sunlight, as it triggered long-lasting allergic reactions. I began losing hair, suffered from intense joint pain, and experienced a low-grade fever that lingered for nearly two years.

The Mumbai doctor suggested I begin steroids. But I asked for some time to think it over. Steroids, as we know, are only a symptomatic treatment — not a cure.

We returned to Gwalior, and around that time, a close friend recommended a renowned homeopath in Delhi.

Most people are sceptical about alternate medicines. But my friend convinced me.

Sometimes, God shows us the right path through a person, a friend, or a situation. We just need to pause, listen, and recognise His voice. In that moment, I felt a quiet certainty — this was the direction I was meant to take. My husband supported me wholeheartedly.

I began homeopathic treatment. Within a few months, my fever reduced from every day to some days in a month.

Allopathy practitioners are often sceptical of alternate medicine — and rightly so in some cases. Quacks exist in every system of healing. That's why it's crucial to find the right person, at the right time, and make the right decision. Much of this clarity comes when we learn to trust our instincts. Our soul always knows what's best for us.

To be doubly sure, my Mumbai doctor suggested getting the homeopathic medicines tested at the ITA Lab in Mumbai — to ensure they didn't contain any hidden steroids. The results came back clean.

I continued the homeopathy treatment for two years. My allergies stopped. My joint pain reduced. Slowly, I began to heal.

Looking back, that period was both frightening and transformative. It taught me the power of listening to my inner voice, even when the world around me leaned heavily on convention. Healing doesn't always come in standard prescriptions — sometimes it comes from quiet conviction, trust, and the courage to explore different paths. That decision, made in faith and supported by love, changed the course of my life.

CHAPTER 15

1988, GWALIOR — A MESSAGE FROM BEYOND

The next few years were filled with frequent travel between Gwalior–Mumbai and Gwalior–Delhi. My doctor in Mumbai needed to monitor my ANA test results every six months. The reports would take nearly ten days, so we often had to stay in Mumbai longer than expected.

On one such trip, we decided to take both our kids to Goa from Mumbai. It was peak season, and we had no reservations. Back then, there were no mobile phones or apps to book hotels instantly.

Fortunately, luck was on our side—we found a room right next to the beach. The children were thrilled and spent hours playing in the sand and surf.

That evening, as the kids and I played at the water's edge, I suddenly realized that one of my rings had slipped off. My heart sank. It wasn't just any ring—it was a simple emerald birthstone ring that my maternal grandmother had given me on my eighth birthday. Small and square, but deeply precious. I always wore it, along with another ring gifted by my sister.

We searched frantically for ten to fifteen minutes. But the waves were relentless, and the sea had swallowed it. I stood quietly for a moment and told myself, *Let it go.* Perhaps it was not meant to stay with me anymore. I closed my eyes and whispered, *"Sorry, Ba. I've lost the only memory I had of you."*

Not wanting to dampen my children's spirits, I decided to let the moment pass and continued playing in the water with them.

About twenty-five minutes later, we were sitting on the shore, backs to the waves, laughing as each wave rushed over us and pulled gently at our bodies. I dug my hands into the wet sand to steady myself whenever a wave hit us. As one big wave crashed and receded, I dug my fingers in the sand to stabilise myself. As the water receded and some of the sand in my fist started slipping away from my closed fist, I felt something solid—my fingers gripped tightly around it instinctively. To my utter astonishment, it felt like the ring.

I gasped.

"The ring… I've found the ring!" I looked at my husband in disbelief, tears welling up in my eyes. Even now, all these years later, I can hardly believe it.

How could something lost in the sea return to me? Was it the angels? My grandmother's spirit? A miracle? Or just a strange coincidence? Who is to know? Some moments in life defy logic.

They remind us that not everything can be explained—and perhaps, not everything needs to be.

Losing that ring felt like losing a part of my past. Finding it again in the vastness of the sea felt like a whisper from the universe, reminding me that what is truly ours never really leaves us. Sometimes, what we let go of with love returns in the most unexpected ways.

Call it grace, call it faith, call it love that transcends time and space—these moments are little miracles that help us believe again.

CHAPTER 16

2004, GWALIOR — THE SILENT LESSONS OF PAIN

Many times, medical science has no explanation for what can't be clinically proven. Unless backed by research and data, alternate medicines are often dismissed. For years, from 1987 to 2007, my annual check-ups in Mumbai all pointed to an autoimmune disease—SLE. Yet, finally, one day, the doctor wrote on my report: *"Not proved."* It was decided that I need not repeat those tests. I was never put on steroids.

And so, life went on.

There were good days and bad. The SLE monster would rear its head every now and then, but I kept moving forward.

After fever and joint pain came pleurisy—an inflammation of the tissues around the lungs. That treatment lasted nine long months in 1991. In 1996, vertigo struck. Each attack meant weeks of medication and rest. The episodes were unpredictable, yet a brain scan showed no abnormalities, so we simply moved on.

For me, these were hiccups—bumps in the road, not dead ends. I joined yoga classes to ease joint pain. I treated every setback as a passing phase. I refused to let illness steal my smile, or my love for travel and life.

Honestly, I told myself: *I'm fine. And I was.* I picked up the threads of life and kept busy with home and started working in the educational field. It was around 1998 Then came 2004.

Just when I thought my battles with health were enough to bear, life tested me in a way I had never imagined.

It was an ordinary day at work when my phone rang. The words on the other end froze everything around me. My daughter, son-in-law, and their two-year-old son had met with a serious accident on their way to Jaipur from Jamnagar.

Without a second thought, we left for Jaipur. That six-hour drive was the longest of my life. The hum of the car engine felt louder than my heartbeat. Every milestone we passed seemed to mock the distance that still lay ahead. I cried the entire way, unable to shake the dread that something irreversible had happened. And it had.

We lost our precious two-year-old grandson.

My daughter was seriously injured. My son-in-law, though physically safe with only minor injuries, was in deep shock. It took nearly two months before my daughter was strong enough to return home with us to Gwalior. Those weeks felt like an endless tunnel of helplessness. There is no word in any language for the loss of a child—perhaps because it is a grief beyond description.

And even though I had no part in it, I somehow felt I had let down my sister in some way. That I had not been able to protect her daughter from this fate.

Some losses change you forever. They leave behind a void that never truly closes. But sometimes, along that broken path, life also brings moments of healing, unexpected guidance, and quiet new beginnings.

I have come to believe that certain events—even the painful ones—arrive to teach us lessons, shift our direction, or awaken a dormant strength. And perhaps, through it all, we are being gently led—not always to answers, but to awareness.

CHAPTER 17

2008, GWALIOR — HELLO? GOD? ARE YOU LISTENING?

Life, in its strange way, continued.

In 2006, my daughter was blessed with twins—a boy and a girl. Their arrival brought a spark of joy back into our lives, a reminder that hope can emerge even from the darkest places. I was blessed to have them with me for one and a half years, as their father was posted in Congo during that time.

Despite setbacks, I continued working. Over the years, I grew as an educationist, helping to set up or improve schools. I served as director in two schools and as an advisor in another until 2012. Thanks to my Mumbai education, I thrived in my chosen field. Later, I also became a certified IELTS trainer and helped many clear the exams.

Life was a juggling act—my work on one side, and on the other, two little angels who filled our days with laughter.

But in the beginning of year 2008, a new shadow quietly entered my life. I began noticing bright flashes of light whenever

I closed my eyes. At first, I ignored them. Then one afternoon, after lunch, my vision blurred slightly. Something felt wrong.

I asked the driver to stop at a nearby ophthalmologist. A series of tests followed. When I picked up the report, one term caught my eye: *Fuchs' Dystrophy.* I had never heard of it.

Confused, I stepped into the doctor's cabin. Another patient was already there, so I stood at the door and asked, "Doctor, what does this mean?" He looked up. "It's a degenerative disease. The corneal cells deteriorate over time, which can eventually lead to blindness."

Stunned, I whispered, "What's the cure?" His answer was brief: "Corneal transplant."

I nodded, thanked him, and walked out. Was I going blind now? Hello? God? Are you listening? In that moment, the world blurred—not because of my eyes, but because of the sudden fear of darkness ahead. And yet, deep inside, a quiet voice whispered: *You've faced storms before. You will find light again.*

Illness may arrive in many forms—some named, some mysterious—but it had not, and would not, define me. I chose to walk forward with hope, even if I had to feel my way through shadows.

Because sometimes, faith sees what the eyes cannot.

CHAPTER 18

2008, GWALIOR — NOTHING TO LOSE

A year after being diagnosed with Fuch's dystrophy, another blow came — I was told I had glaucoma too. A glaucoma expert visiting the eye hospital I regularly consulted was called in for a second opinion. After examining me, he confirmed the diagnosis and recommended a laser operation **the very next morning**. He was scheduled to return to Delhi the following day, so there was a sense of urgency.

My surgery was scheduled for 7 a.m. I remember going home, feeling unsettled. Something about the speed of it all didn't sit right with me. I recalled reading somewhere that laser-operated eyes were not ideal candidates for corneal transplants in the future — a serious concern given my Fuch's dystrophy.

I set my alarm for 6 a.m., trying to convince myself that I was overthinking. But when the alarm rang, I sat up in bed with a sudden clarity. *I'm not ready for this. I need another opinion.*

I turned to my husband and said firmly, "I'm not going through with the operation. I want a third opinion."

To my surprise, he didn't argue.

I called the hospital and cancelled the procedure.

Soon after, I began searching for the best glaucoma specialist in Delhi. I found one — highly reputed — and managed to get an appointment. We made the trip. After a thorough examination, he confirmed the presence of glaucoma but said, *"There is no urgent need for surgery right now."* I felt relieved — not just about avoiding a premature procedure, but also about trusting my instincts.

Back in Gwalior, I dove deep into research.

I began exploring alternative treatments for eye conditions. That's when I came across an Ayurvedic eye hospital based in Kerala. To my luck, they held periodic consultations in Delhi for patients from the northern parts of the country.

I quickly booked an appointment.

On the day of the consultation, my husband and I arrived at the Delhi centre. The place was overflowing with people — patients from the North, Northeast, some even from the border regions. While waiting, I struck up conversations with two old patients. Both had been written off by allopathic medicine, and yet, they were showing signs of improvement through this treatment. Their stories gave me hope.

When my name was called, I entered a small room where two assistant doctors and a senior Ayurvedic practitioner were seated. The senior doctor didn't speak Hindi or English. The assistants asked questions on his behalf and translated my answers.

He examined my eyes briefly with a torch and that was it — no machines, no scans.

I was instructed to collect my medicines from the counter outside.

As we left the centre, my husband looked unconvinced. "He couldn't even speak properly," he said. "How's he going to treat you?"

I paused, looked at him, and replied calmly,

"I have nothing to lose."

That morning on the day of my scheduled operation, when the alarm rang, it didn't just wake me — it woke up something deeper inside me.

A knowing, not loud, but certain.

We often seek answers outside — in experts, in machines, in second and third opinions. But sometimes, the truest guidance comes from within. That inner voice, born from lived experience, intuition, and quiet reflection, rarely screams — it whispers.

The decision to pause the procedure wasn't about defiance. It was about trust — not in a system or a doctor, but in myself.

In the end, perhaps healing begins the moment we start listening — not just to doctors or diagnosis, but to the voice we've long ignored: our own.

At the end of the same year in 2008 my son got married.

From 2004 to 2008

There were high notes— the joy of becoming a mother-in-law and gaining another daughter. Mom's visit from Canada.

And there were low notes, supporting a loved one through alcoholism, and facing injustice at work.

Yet, with the birth of our fourth grandchild, life gently turned a new corner—towards **Pune.**

CHAPTER 19

2009, GWALIOR — MIRACLES OF LIFE

"When the body stops listening, the soul begins to whisper. Healing begins when we learn to listen again."

– My reflections, 1991

It had been almost a year since I was taking the ayurvedic medicines.

My corneal cell count was stagnant. It had stopped deteriorating further. My Delhi doctor was surprised to see the tests. Glaucoma was non-existent. It was like a miracle had taken place.

I think we have an innate ability to know what can heal us and also the ability to heal ourselves with positive thoughts. The most important thing is not to get intimidated by the diagnosis.

Fear can prevent us from healing. Our thoughts can become our worst enemy.

Our diagnosis may be our destiny but how much and how long we suffer is our choice.

I truly believe our instincts tell us what is right for us. We need to just be able to tune into our instincts.

We all have it. Only some know how to tune in.

Though we all can tune in. Practicing meditation helps us turn inward. It helps us to listen to our inner calling.

Even when we do something wrong, our inner voice tells us, 'Boss this isn't right.' But, when we don't pay attention to it, it stops communicating with us.

Another important thing is to be able to let go of anything or anyone that doesn't serve us. We carry unnecessary burdens on our shoulders. We are all actually going towards the same destination. It's just that for some of us, the road is a bit bumpier than others. Enjoy the ride.

My journey continued. Sometimes more bumpy than other times.

In December 2008, my son got married in Pune. And in 2012, we welcomed our fourth grandchild, a granddaughter, into the world. It was decided that I would shift to Pune to help take care of her, as both her parents were working. It felt like a new purpose had been handed to me — to nurture, to support, to be there.

I still remember the day she was born. When they brought her out and put her in a cradle outside the delivery room. They called us to see her. We were four of us waiting outside. Her maternal grandmother parents and my husband and me.

Her eyes were closed when we went in. As we stood gazing at her in wonderment, she opened her eyes and literally looked at each one of us in the eye. One by one she checked us all out. I was standing third. She literally held my gaze before moving on to check the last person, her grandfather.

In my entire life, I have not seen a newborn baby make such deliberate eye contact.

It is rightly said that grandchildren are a blessing from heaven. I enjoyed each moment with each of my grandchildren to the fullest. Grateful to God for these beautiful moments.

My Fuch's dystrophy had stabilised, however, my vertigo episodes worsened. After several consultations, neurologists diagnosed me with Ménière's disease — another autoimmune condition, one that affects the inner ear and causes hearing loss and dizzy spells.

I remember thinking, *Another ailment? Really?* It felt like my body was a silent battlefield, collecting invisible wars one by one.

Believe me, I chose to totally ignore this diagnosis and SLE in general. I pretended I had no health issues. And I felt normal except when I had vertigo attacks. I was busy taking care of my youngest grandchild and was enjoying every moment of it. I forgot all my ailments when with her.

The more my health pushed me down the more active I became. I travelled, hiked and did 10 km marathons. It was as if I wanted to disregard any health issues.

Then one day, my aunt came to visit us in Pune. In passing, she mentioned a homeopathic doctor in Mumbai who had been helping her. Something about it stirred a quiet instinct in me — a gentle nudge from within. I travelled to Mumbai and consulted the doctor. To my relief and surprise, her medicines worked. My years of debilitating vertigo attacks stopped with homeopathic medicine.

Just like that, a door I didn't even know existed opened.

Had I not moved to Pune, I may never have met this doctor. It felt like a quiet affirmation: sometimes, life puts us in places not by accident, but by quiet design.

CHAPTER 20

2010, GWALIOR — MEDITATION, MIGRAINE & A MIRACLE

In the quiet corners of time, Lie moments we once passed by—

Unseen, unheard, unnamed, Yet waiting for their why.

What felt like fragments once, Lost in life's hurried stream, Return one day as meaning, In the echo of a dream.

Life often doesn't take us where we *want* to go, but quietly guides us to where we *need* to be.

I'd always had a spiritual bend, a quiet curiosity about the unseen threads that run beneath life. Life was going on as usual, when a casual acquaintance mentioned she was part of an organisation called *The Art of Living and I should enrol in their basic course.* So I decided to give it a try.

The first course felt good. Uplifting even. But like many, I didn't continue with the follow-ups.

Life picked up pace again.

A couple of years later, I was back in Gwalior from Pune for some work she again insisted I try the *Advanced Course*.

"This teacher is special," she said, "He's not a local teacher. You must attend his course."

I signed up. It was a four-day program, filled with deep teachings on living a more joyful, present, and meaningful life. The teacher had a magnetic presence—calm yet powerful, wise yet warm. His voice held a devotion that stirred something deep inside. The bhajans he sang weren't just songs—they were experiences. He had beautiful, thick, flowing hair and looked majestic in his white robes.

He spoke on various aspects of how to live a more fulfilled life.

Each day, we explored new forms of meditation. The programme focused on deeper meditation techniques, including Sudarshan Kriya, pranayama, and rejuvenating yoga, alongside guided meditations and periods of silence. The program aimed to help participants achieve a meditative state effortlessly, experience deep rest, and gain a deeper understanding of themselves and their emotions.

But what truly struck me was how he seemed to *read minds*. I'd think something—and he'd speak of it, as if in answer, from the stage.

It was uncanny. Comforting, yet a little unsettling too.

Two of the four days were spent in silence. At first, I found it awkward. Then—something shifted.

The silence wasn't empty.

It was *full.*

Full of forgotten feelings. Full of space. Full of stillness.

It became a doorway to a part of myself I had never met.

One of those days, a migraine hit me. They often did. I felt drawn to him—without thought—and bowed before him. He gently placed his hand on my head and I could feel heat radiating into me. He whispered softly, *"Drink water."*

That was all.

And just like that—*my headache vanished.*

What was that energy? I can't explain it. I only know what I felt.

After that course, I began meditating regularly. My practice deepened. Slowly, almost unknowingly, I found myself sitting for longer, sinking deeper.

Sometimes, there would be a moment of utter stillness—a silence so complete, it felt like I had dipped into a vast, endless ocean. It was blissful, like the calm after a long-needed sleep.

One evening, I meditated for more than two hours. My husband, worried, gently shook me—*"What are you doing? Something may happen to you,"* he said.

Strangely, after that day, I could never reach that depth again. Never experienced that same moment of blissful silence.

And to this day—I don't know *why.*

CHAPTER 21

2015, PUNE — UNDEFEATED

Three years after the birth of my granddaughter, my father-in-law passed away and my husband decided to shift to Pune. My mother-in-law also moved with us. Having lived in Gwalior for over sixty years, the change could have been unsettling for her. But hats off to her — she adapted to this new city with grace and ease.

We bought an apartment close to my son's, so I could continue babysitting my granddaughter. Me moving out of my son's home was a painful affair for my little granddaughter. Her five-year-old mind could not understand why things had to change. Yet, each day brought us back together. After school, we would pick her up, and she would spend her afternoons at our house — playing, chattering, filling the rooms with her presence. In the evenings, when her mother returned from work, she would go back to her own home.

My mother-in-law was a three-time cancer warrior. Each time, she fought fiercely and came out stronger. Eventually, she passed away at the age of eighty-eight, not from cancer, but due to a cardiac arrest — a woman of remarkable willpower and quiet strength.

In Pune, she developed a small cut on the second toe of her foot that refused to heal. The doctors told us the veins in her lower leg had thinned out, causing very poor blood circulation — likely a delayed side effect of the urethral cancer treatment she had undergone nearly a decade earlier.

The diagnosis was dry gangrene. The doctors recommended amputation of the toe. But she didn't want to go through that, and I wholeheartedly supported her decision. It just didn't make sense to me — if a small wound wasn't healing, how could we expect an amputation to recover?

Respecting our wishes, the doctor suggested we call a nurse daily to clean and dress the wound. For a few days, we did that. But the wound seemed to ooze more than before.

Then I took over.

Every single day, with complete dedication, I would clean the wound and gently squeeze out the white pus. She never once complained of pain.

As months turned into years, to everyone's surprise — especially the doctors — the gangrene began to reverse. It never fully healed, but it looked far better than before.

Till her last day in September 2017, my mother-in-law remained fiercely independent. In fact, just two hours before she passed, she walked into the ICU on her own.

A pillar of strength and dignity. Her quiet resilience, her stoic spirit — we will always carry her memory in our hearts.

Her life taught us that real strength is not loud — it is quiet, steady, and deeply rooted in self-belief. She showed us that aging with dignity is possible when one chooses courage over fear, and grace over complaint. She didn't fight life; she flowed with it, choosing acceptance over resistance.

Even in pain, she chose independence. Even in illness, she chose dignity. Her journey reminds us that healing isn't always about curing the body — sometimes, it's about nurturing the soul and honouring the choices of the heart.

Her legacy is a simple but profound truth:

Live with purpose, suffer with grace, and leave with peace.

Her departure in September 2017 left an emptiness in our lives, yet her presence lingered quietly in our hearts. I thought her final lesson to us was about strength, grace, and acceptance. But I was yet to discover that love does not always end with death — sometimes, it chooses to stay back, unseen yet deeply felt.

CHAPTER 22

2017, PUNE — A MOTHER'S SOUL

"Some goodbyes are not spoken.

Some souls linger — not out of fear, but out of love."

My son drove me and my husband to the hospital at nine in the morning. My husband had pain in his abdomen. A simple appendix case, we thought. But the hospital delayed surgery until 6 p.m. — nine whole hours of sheer negligence.

The surgery left him weak, drained, and far from recovered. He stayed there for ten nights, during which the wound on the outside seemed fine, but the inside told a different story. The doctors kept wavering — "We will discharge today," then "No, not yet."

I watched him lose weight, strength, and spirit in front of my eyes.

By the tenth day, I had lost all faith in the hospital and the surgeon. Something felt very wrong. I demanded a discharge and brought him home.

That morning, I had told my mother-in-law he would be discharged by afternoon. But the hospital formalities delayed the discharge until late evening. Worried, my mother-in-law called to ask what time we would be getting home — but there was something in her voice. A hollowness. A fatigue I couldn't ignore.

Something in me felt deeply unsettled. I immediately called the man who came home to collect her blood samples as and when required. Despite the late hour, he agreed to come that very evening.

The next day, her reports came in — RBC count was dangerously low. We rushed her to her consulting physician. He said we needed to admit her to the hospital and give her blood. The next day, he wanted to perform an endoscopy.

I had a nagging feeling that she would not come back from the hospital. I asked him if the blood could be given at home without admitting her. I suggested that I would bring her to the hospital for the endoscopy after the blood transfusion at home. But he said it was not possible, as they had no such provision.

We admitted her in the evening. That night, she passed away.

Despite the pain from his surgery, my husband stood tall — emotionally, if not physically. He performed all the rituals, the final duties a son must do. Even in weakness, he honoured her.

Four days later, he collapsed again.

This time, we didn't take a chance. My son researched. A new hospital. A new doctor. A new hope.

An MRI showed the horror we feared — an internal perforation near the operated area. Immediate surgery was the only option.

I locked up the house and stayed with him at the hospital. It had been just five days since we lost my mother-in-law.

The next morning, I returned home briefly to make some semi-solid food for my husband. It was 10 a.m.

As I opened the door, I felt her.

Not in a vision. Not in a dream. But in something far more powerful — her presence.

A sudden wave of scent — her almond-scented hair oil, the sharp tinge of her daily medicines, the warmth of a life recently departed — wrapped around me.

I took a step back. A chill ran through me. I almost waited outside for the house help who was supposed to arrive.

And then I whispered to myself, "She's not here to harm. She's here because her son isn't okay."

At that moment, the fear melted.

I entered the house. The heaviness lifted. She had made her presence known… and then silently stepped back.

Over the next few days, every time I entered the house, there would be a faint, familiar scent in the air.

Until one day, it was gone.

Some souls do not depart immediately.

They linger — not because they're lost, but because love isn't done yet.

My mother-in-law stayed back for her son, just a little longer.

Not in form, but in essence.

In scent. In presence. In care.

I believe she waited… until he was safe.

Only then did she truly leave.

CHAPTER 23

2019, PUNE — HELD BY LIGHT

'A whisper from the divine before the storm is born.

Where fear once lived, now walks faith.'

By now, we were well settled in Pune. My life revolved around caring for my granddaughter and managing the home. I wasn't involved in the Art of Living or any spiritual practices at the time.

But one early morning, I had a vivid dream.

In the dream, I saw **Sri Sri Ravi Shankar ji**, surrounded by a peaceful, radiant light. He was smiling gently, his palms extended upwards toward me as he said,

"Come with me. You have nothing to fear. I am there with you."

And I place both my hands in his hands. Feeling peaceful.

We were surrounded by clouds — soft, white, almost otherworldly. I instinctively knew he was referring to the soul leaving the material world. The moment was so blissful, words truly fell short.

The dream startled me awake. It was early morning. I got up, and stood at the window, still wrapped in the presence of what I had just experienced.

What was that? I thought. *Why did it feel so real?*

It wasn't just a dream. It was **a visitation**.

For the first time in my life, **I felt no fear of death**. Something that had always terrified me now felt... peaceful. It felt like I had touched the other side and come back with serenity.

But one thing puzzled me — I had never met Guruji. I wasn't his follower, didn't have his photo, and hadn't watched his discourses. Then **why** did he come to me in a dream? I was soon to find out.

I shared the dream with my husband. "I don't think I fear death anymore," I said softly. He, in his usual way, dismissed it casually. But something within me had shifted permanently.

A few days later, I noticed something strange — my face looked slightly asymmetric. One side appeared a little droopy. I also felt a subtle imbalance while walking or bending. Then one day, I had the *weirdest* experience.

I was out driving, and suddenly — I couldn't remember the gears.

Which one was first? Which was second? Or third? It was as if my brain had momentarily gone blank.

I pulled over and stared at the gear lever, trying to make sense of the markings.

After a few moments, I restarted the car — but now I couldn't recall whether I was in second or third gear.

I somehow made it back home, a little shaken and confused.

It wasn't dramatic, but it was *just enough* to raise a red flag.

Something wasn't right.

My internal antennae went up.

It was time to consult a doctor.

We went to a neurophysician. After the examination, he said gently,

"There's nothing urgent, but I suggest you get a brain MRI whenever you can."

As we stepped out of the OPD, my husband said, "We don't have anything else to do right now. Let's check with radiology — maybe they have an empty slot."

They did.

I went in for the MRI. My husband waited outside.

Half an hour later, the technician returned. Calmly, he questioned me,

"What problems are you having? There's a tiny tumour in your brain."

My immediate response? "Oh shit!"

Haha! I don't think I had used that phrase since school days! And yet — surprisingly — I felt **no panic. No fear. Nothing.**

Just... **acceptance.**

In that moment, I realized:

My Guru had already walked me through this.

He had entered my life without noise or drama, quietly preparing me for what was to come — filling me with strength, grace, and dignity.

What I thought was a mere dream turned out to be a sacred preparation.

Guruji didn't just visit me;

He walked ahead of me, lighting the path I didn't know I would soon take.

That morning, fear left me. And in its place came trust.

Because when grace arrives uninvited, it means you are already being held.

CHAPTER 24

2019, PUNE — HUSBANDS CAN BE RIGHT TOO!! ☺

And then began a series of consultations. Some doctors recommended immediate surgery. Others advised a 'wait and watch' approach. But they all agreed on one terrifying thing — it was a malignancy.

One surgeon even suggested an immediate operation *while I would be fully awake and talking during the procedure*. Since the tumour was deep-seated, he explained, being conscious could help him avoid critical areas of the brain.

Yes, you heard that right — **awake brain surgery**.

Also known as an *awake craniotomy*, it's a neurosurgical procedure where the patient remains awake during parts of the operation. Local anaesthesia numbs the scalp, and the patient may be lightly sedated — but they're conscious and able to respond, helping the surgeon avoid vital areas during tumour removal or epilepsy treatment.

Believe me, I ran as fast as I could from that one!

Just the thought was **shit scary** — pardon my language! 😂

So I did what any terrified-yet-resilient person would do — I researched. I looked up some of the top surgeons in India. The best ones down South felt too far for regular follow-ups, so I chose a renowned one in Mumbai. He suggested we wait and watch. A less aggressive approach.

Every three months, I had to undergo an MRI — but not before a blood test to check the kidney function, as an intravenous dye was injected for clarity of the MRI. Each MRI session took nearly two hours, and the entire routine became a part of my life.

After three or four quarterly scans, the doctor was satisfied enough to shift to six-monthly MRIs. That brought some relief.

Around this time, something within me changed.

I started meditating more regularly than ever before.

But now, there was a *difference* — a *guru* had entered my life.

My faith deepened. My affirmations grew stronger.

I felt as though I was being *hand-held* by an invisible force — a power I had never known before.

In the middle of all this uncertainty, I made a bold move — I opened a pre-school.

Yes, despite my medical condition, despite strong opposition from my husband.

I chose to ignore my diagnosis the way I had ignored my SLE… and my husband! 😄

But as life often reminds us — *not every brave step leads to success.*

I launched the school in January 2020… and by March 2020, COVID hit.

It was a complete disaster for my new venture.

And in that moment of crashing dreams, I had to admit —

Once in a while, your husband could be right too!!!

Hahaha!

CHAPTER 25

2020, PUNE — FAITH OVER FEAR: A LOCKDOWN JOURNEY

Like the rest of the world, we too shut ourselves indoors during the COVID-19 pandemic. No maids, no outside food, and every online purchase was meticulously disinfected. It was the strangest time in my life—a surreal stillness wrapped in anxiety.

The hardest part? Not being able to see my granddaughter. Though she lived just a stone's throw away, we didn't meet for several months when cases were at their peak. That distance felt heavier than miles.

Even going for my routine brain MRI felt like inviting danger. But with God's grace, we all stayed safe.

To do something constructive with my time and to uplift my spirits, I turned to painting—and to my surprise, discovered I was actually good at it. I even sold a few paintings, and each sale felt like a small miracle, boosting my confidence when the world outside was crumbling.

As travel remained restricted, I began consulting my Mumbai-based neurosurgeon online. This time, however, he suggested we should consider surgery.

I wasn't ready—not mentally, at least. I felt physically okay and couldn't imagine going through brain surgery amidst a global health crisis.

He understood but gave me a condition: instead of six-monthly MRIs, I was now required to get one done every three months once again.

Not entirely convinced, I sought a second opinion from a renowned neurosurgeon in Delhi. Traveling to Delhi during COVID was no easy feat, but we managed—staying at a relative's empty home where their staff still lived. We didn't dine out or socialize; COVID had planted fear deep into everyone's hearts.

The Delhi doctor had me undergo another MRI at his hospital, with his trusted radiologist. He compared it with a previous scan done a few months before. Seeing very little change between the two, he recommended we take the *wait and watch* route, with six-monthly MRI follow-ups.

That's when my spiritual journey intensified.

I began meditating, chanting, affirming, manifesting with deep faith in my Guruji, Sri Sri Ravishankar.

Slowly, my MRIs moved from six-monthly to annual follow-ups. I chose—deliberately, and often—to forget I had been diagnosed with a brain malignancy.

I began living.

I travelled internationally. I painted. I prayed—manifested that I would never need brain surgery. The very thought still terrified me.

My faith deepened. I was no longer living in fear. I was living in faith. My Guruji was walking with me.

CHAPTER 26

2022, PUNE — GRIEF BRINGS CANCER

My mom was not keeping well. It had been four years since I had met her. Though we spoke every day, it was not the same as meeting in person.

Our call times were a funny ritual. It was so difficult to make her focus the camera on herself during our calls. Sometimes, I would be talking to the ceiling, sometimes to her feet. On lucky days, I would get to see her face. But I never ever told her about me having a malignancy in the brain. There was no point in disturbing her peace of mind in her old age. Besides, what good could have come out of telling her something like this?

I so badly wanted to visit her in Canada, but circumstances didn't allow it. Post-COVID, visas were getting delayed endlessly.

Four days after she passed away, I received my visa.

It was heartbreaking. There are no words to describe that kind of pain.

My mom was my heartbeat. My lifeline.

It felt as though a part of me had died with her.

I somehow lost the will to live. I longed to see her—even if it was in the afterlife.

When you're in deep mourning, your focus shifts away from wellness.

You stop being grateful for the life God has given you.

You begin to surrender the desire to live.

And sometimes, God shows you just how precious life is—in the harshest way.

One morning, I felt a lump in my right breast.

I consulted a gynaecologist, who suggested I go for a mammogram.

The very next day, we went in. Immediately after the mammogram, the technician asked me to wait—she wanted to consult the radiologist. A few minutes later, she returned and said the radiologist would be doing a sono-mammogram as there was a lump they needed to examine more closely.

During the sono-mammogram, the radiologist advised me to meet a breast oncologist right away and get a biopsy done.

The biopsy was scheduled. The reports confirmed a malignancy.

I was in disbelief.

I sent the samples to Tata Memorial Hospital in Mumbai, and the diagnosis was reconfirmed.

I was shell-shocked.

How could I possibly have two different types of cancer in two different parts of my body—at the same time? I had never even heard of something like this.

I tried to joke with myself—maybe because I had prayed so hard and feared so much for the brain cancer to go away, God had shifted the monster from my br-ain to my br-east! 😄

But it's truly said—you only begin to value your life when you're at the brink of losing it.

And I found myself saying to God:

"God, I know I said I don't want to live anymore… but you don't need to take everything I say so seriously!!!" 😂😂

When life brings you to your knees, it's only so you value it and rise again—stronger, clearer, and more alive than ever.

CHAPTER 27

2022, PUNE — A MOMENT OUTSIDE MY BODY

I was scheduled for surgery two weeks later. A partial mastectomy had been decided, to be followed by eight cycles of chemotherapy and 20 sessions of radiation.

I was surprisingly calm and went smiling into the operation theatre. My faith in the Supreme Power and Guruji gave me that inner strength.

The operating table was unlike anything I had ever seen. It was shaped like a cross—very slim, with no space to rest your arms except on the horizontal sides of the crossbar.

A few medical staff were around me, attaching machines and checking my vitals while waiting for the anaesthetist and my oncologist to arrive.

As I lay there, open from the waist up, my arms stretched on either side and no cloth covering my upper torso, a strange calm washed over me. I thought to myself, I'm lying down like Christ had, on his cross. I felt a sense of freedom lying open and spoke quietly to myself,

"Chalo chale." *(Let's go.)* And then… something surreal happened.

I was suddenly **floating**, but very close to my body. There was an **indescribable sense of peace**—so deep and still, I can't find words for it. I wasn't high up near the ceiling, just a little above my body, watching everything from a low angle.

I could see the nurse attaching something to check my vitals. I heard her say, "There's no pulse."

The technician replied, "Put it on yourself and check the instrument."

She said, "I've already done that."

Then he turned to someone and said, "See if the machine is off."

Another voice answered, "No, it's on."

Then he said, **"Go call the doctor."**

I saw the nurse rushing out.

And just like that, **I was back in my body.**

What was that? I don't know.

When I woke up from the anaesthesia that afternoon, I remembered every moment of it clearly. But I didn't mention it to anyone. I thought maybe it was a dream… or a hallucination.

However, later that evening, a male nurse came into my room and spoke with my son. He explained to my son that **all my parameters had changed**, and they suspected it was due to something injected just before the operation. That's when I realized that what I had experienced **was not a dream**. It had really happened.

That night, my daughter-in-law stayed back with me at the hospital. She was so vigilant that even if I turned, she would ask me if I needed anything.

The next night, my husband was with me at night and as the room became silent with only the sounds of the night, I shared my experience with my husband, unsure of how he would receive it. I asked him, **"Will you believe me if I tell you something strange?"** He listened quietly as I described it all. And surprisingly, he didn't express any disbelief.

I still don't know what that was for sure. It's mind-boggling for me even today. Did that really happen? Did my soul leave my body for a few seconds at will? Or was it a delusion? I'll never know. But the peace I felt in that moment… That was real.

Perhaps in that moment, I wasn't dying—I was simply being reminded that I'm more than just this body.

Call it science, spirit, or simply the unknown—what happened that day was real to me, and maybe that's all that matters.

CHAPTER 28

2023, PUNE — THE BATTLE BEGINS

I honestly believe that operation is the easy part of cancer treatment.

The true battle begins later — with the demonic monster called chemotherapy. It doesn't just attack cancer cells. It prowls deeper, testing your will, your spirit, and even the fragile vanity you thought you could protect.

The first challenge was finding a vein. Several pricks later, one surrendered. And then came the first chemo — like a tsunami, violent and unstoppable. Vertigo, vomiting, weakness… all crashing over me in one force.

We left home at eight in the morning and returned at ten-thirty at night. I had walked into the hospital, but I came out in a wheelchair — the world tilting, my legs unwilling to hold me.

My husband suffered in silence, watching me unravel.

For days after, I barely had the energy to speak. Nausea made food an enemy, yet I knew I had to eat. Slowly, I would make my way to the dining table, instructing my new cook how to make soup, curd rice, or whatever I might manage to eat.

And, I missed my mom, every day, every minute.

I was fortunate to have an excellent chemo oncologist and a compassionate health care team. My doctor warned me: after the first chemo, my hair would fall. And it did. In clumps, in handfuls — like autumn leaves letting go without asking my permission.

My hair had always been my indulgence. Hair spas, best hair stylists, particular cut, gentle dyes — my small ritual of vanity. And now it was slipping away, strand by strand.

After my second chemo, my doctor suggested I shave it off for hygiene. A week later, I told my husband I was ready. He called a barber to our home. I sat in the balcony, calm, resigned. Just as the first razor sweep was about to demolish my remaining hair, the doorbell rang. My son and daughter-in-law stood there. My husband had called them for moral support.

The moment I saw my son, my calm shattered. I broke down, sobbing uncontrollably — and then, never again. That day, I cried for my hair, my old self, and the part of me that had changed forever.

Losing my hair was not just an act of hygiene. It was an initiation — a lesson in impermanence. Our looks, our possessions, our bodies… all are passing visitors. Only the self beneath remains.

Hair, I learned, is only ever on loan. It grows, it shines, it falls, it disappears. But the self beneath — the will to endure, to love, to keep walking — remains untouched. Cancer had stripped away what I thought I could not live without, only to reveal what could never be taken: the quiet, unyielding light within.

CHAPTER 29

2023, PUNE — THE ALIEN IN THE MIRROR

My hand was black and blue in places where the chemo was administered. Before the third chemo, it was decided that I needed a port. A port is a device inserted inside your shoulder and attached to a vein to make the chemo procedure easy. This procedure can be done under local anaesthesia, but my surgeon decided to do it under general anaesthesia.

So, just within two months, I was back in the operation theatre. But, this time, I did not say to myself, "chalo chale"

Hahaha!!

After the third chemo, I lost my eyebrows and my eyelashes. Now this was something I had not heard of. So I was quite taken aback to see a completely hairless alien in the mirror.

I also lost my taste buds. Everything tasted like mud. Actually, maybe mud is tastier too.

On chemo days, I would roll a ghee-laced roti (Indian flat bread) with banana and eat.

One chocolate too. Sweet tasted better than savoury.

The port was near the shoulder, hence a taste of the medications given would come in the throat, making me feel nauseous. To combat that, I would keep popping a cardamom or a mint chewing gum.

I was blessed that the 'Bhagavad Gita' had come into my life just before my chemotherapy. I believe when a Guru comes into your life, he ensures your destined path becomes easier. He quietly guides you towards what is best for you. And my Guru was walking every step with me.

A neighbour shared a link to free online classes by Gita Parivar. I decided to try it out. I had never learnt Sanskrit, but I believe it's never too late to try something new. The way they taught and explained, after a few sessions, I was hooked on it. It gave me a purpose. It gave me strength and resilience.

The chemo brain fog made it a bit more challenging, but I was not ready to give up. It was something that held me together during that crazy time. The only thing that gave me a sense of normalcy

With the port inserted, they broke my one chemo session into three parts. That way, they could give me a maximum dosage of chemotherapy medication. But it also meant more visits to the day care. More chemo sessions. Eighteen more chemotherapy sessions besides the two full ones.

That's when I took a call to stop being a burden on my husband, my caretaker. I requested him to just drop me off at the day care centre in the morning and come back in the evening to do the hospital formalities and take me home.

I would keep myself busy painting, taking my one-hour online Bhagavad Gita class or watching a downloaded movie on my granddaughter's iPad during chemotherapy sessions.

Cancer does not just take a toll on the patient's life; it affects and takes a toll on the entire family. People who care for us. When we bring ourselves to conduct with resilience, we help our caregivers. We give them a respite from their ordeal of dealing with a cancer patient.

CHAPTER 30

2023, PUNE — WHEN CHALLENGES ARE CHALLENGED

During one of my chemo sessions, I began feeling a tingling sensation in my legs. Soon, they felt numb to the touch. My chemo oncologist suggested we consult a neurophysician. Upon examination, he advised an **electromyography** (**EMG**) and **nerve conduction study** (**NCS**) to check for nerve damage—a known side effect of chemotherapy.

The chemo was halted, and I was wheeled to the testing room. These electrodiagnostic tests measure the electrical activity of muscles and the speed at which signals travel along nerves, helping identify the location and extent of damage.

The EMG involved inserting a thin needle electrode into my muscles to record electrical activity at rest and during contraction. Damaged muscles can show abnormal signals, revealing nerve dysfunction. The NCS sent a small electric current through each nerve—every time they tested one, my legs shook involuntarily. I stopped counting after a while how many times the current was passed.

Thankfully, the results showed my nerves were **not extensively damaged**.

Still, I was now living with a tongue that could not taste and legs that felt like rubber.

My legs tired easily, so my husband arranged for someone to give me light massages daily, hoping to improve circulation and reduce the numbness. The neurophysician prescribed medication in the hope of reversing the damage.

Meanwhile, my fingernails and toenails slowly turned dark blue. When I expressed concern, my oncologist said, "Put on some nail paint and forget about it." At one point, my nails looked like they had permanent blue polish—*haha!* It took nearly a year for the discolouration to grow out.

After a few more chemo sessions, angry red rashes appeared on my feet. I was referred to a skin specialist. That's when I mentioned my long-standing autoimmune condition, which I had barely noted in my case history. A blood test confirmed it was still present. My oncologist suggested I consult a specialist for it. I told him,

"Please, sir, I have chosen to forget about it for the past thirty years. I'd like to continue to do so. Right now, my only focus is on my cancer treatment and recovery."

He didn't insist—something I'm still grateful for.

The allergy took a long time to heal. The skin peeled, making it look ugly. Now I had red feet with blackish blue nails. I had become colourful and hairless!! But the allergy healed eventually, just before my 60th birthday!! I had always dreamed of celebrating my 60th birthday with friends and family. Despite my condition, I went ahead with the plan. I organised it myself from my home. Venue, cake, decoration. Everything. I even hand-painted coasters as gifts for my guests.

Friends and family members travelled from different cities. Their presence made me feel deeply loved and special. Yes, it was tiring, but I fulfilled my dream.

When God gives us challenges, He also gives us the strength to face them.

Challenges do not mean we give up on our dreams. **Live your dreams today—there are no postponements in life.**

I celebrated not because life was easy, but because it was hard. In raising a toast on my 60th, I was raising a flag—declaring that joy will not surrender to illness.

The body may falter, but the spirit refuses. In the middle of numb legs and tired days, I found that fulfilling dreams are not luxuries—they are medicine for the soul.

Even when my legs trembled and my taste had vanished, my heart still knew the flavour of joy. I learned that life's finest celebrations are not postponed until we are whole—they are the very moments that make us whole.

CHAPTER 31

2023, PUNE — MORE THAN MEDICINE

Amidst my chemotherapy sessions, I got to know that Guruji was visiting Pune after many years.

He was in Pune at a time when my body felt weakest. My heart longed for one thing—Darshan of my Guruji, Sri Sri Ravishankar ji, but I was too unwell to go into a large crowd. I felt deeply upset that I wouldn't be able to see him. I had never met him before, and yet I yearned for it desperately.

On his last night in Pune, I silently said in my heart, *"Guruji, you don't want to meet me? You've come here after so many years, and that too when I am so unwell, unable to come and see you."*

The next morning, my phone rang. It was my first cousin from Kolhapur, who also has a house in Pune. She said, "Sangita, this evening Guruji is coming to our house for a short while. Please come and take his blessings since you are not well. It will be only family, so you should be comfortable. But come on time, he won't be here long—he has to leave soon after."

My cousin had no idea I was his follower. We had never even spoken about it, and yet she thought of me.

Coincidence? Maybe.

But just like that, I received my Guru Darshan.

I felt so blessed. I could not utter a single word—only tears of joy and gratitude flowed down my cheeks as I saw him being welcomed by my cousin and her family. When I finally stood before him, I simply fell at his feet. In that moment, I knew everything was going to be alright.

That blessing gave me the strength to face what lay ahead.

On the last day of chemotherapy, my doctor told me to return in a week for a follow-up and asked if I had any questions. Without hesitation, I asked, "How soon can I travel?"

I actually saw his jaw drop. After a pause, he replied, "Two weeks of rest first. Then radiation—Monday to Friday, for thirty days, twenty sittings. After that, rest for one month… and then you can travel."

That was all I needed to hear. My school batchmates and I began planning a trip for when my recovery period was over.

In the meantime, I started walking every day. Ten minutes at first, then twenty. Gradually, thirty… and eventually forty minutes. With every step, my stamina and my confidence returned.

Towards the end of chemo, my brother and sister-in-law came to visit. I hadn't seen my brother in seven years and we had not met since Mom passed away.

One evening, we went to a friend's house for dinner. On the way back, my head began to spin. As soon as I reached home, I vomited before I could even reach the washroom.

Normally, I would quietly clean up after myself. But that night, my brother—calm, steady, without a word—cleaned the mess for me.

That was probably the second time I cried my heart out during my treatment. I hugged my brother and cried. I cried for the burden I felt I had become. I cried for the seven years of distance between us. And I cried for the unexpected comfort of being cared for. It was as if the walls I had built around my pain suddenly cracked open.

Exactly one month after finishing radiation—and another month of rest—I boarded a flight to Kashmir with my friends.

The mountains rose like silent guardians, the air was crisp with the scent of pine, and the rivers sang over stones polished by time. I wandered through valleys, gazed at snow-kissed peaks, and even dared the zip line.

In those moments, I wasn't a patient. I wasn't a survivor.

I was simply alive.

Healing came to me in many forms—through my Guru's grace, my husband's unwavering support, my brother's quiet love, and the mountains that reminded me how to live again.

CHAPTER 32

2024, PUNE — A CALL FROM BEYOND?

Life began picking up pace. But my hair… it was stubborn. It came back painfully slow — or perhaps it only felt that way to me. Even after a year of treatment, it looked like a crew cut — short, grey, and unexpectedly curly.

My routine had changed. My eating habits had changed. I became more conscious of what I was putting into my body. The biscuits and bakery treats I once loved no longer tempted me. Processed food had moved to the very bottom of my list. In their place came fresh fruits, colourful vegetables, and nourishing meals.

Meditation became my anchor. I practiced gratitude and affirmed my healing daily. Pranayama was now an everyday ritual, and I believe that helped my BP medicine to be reduced to the bare minimum.

A quiet calmness began to settle over me.

My faith in Guruji deepened with every passing day. It truly felt as though he was guiding me, step by step. I started reading one Adhyay of the *Bhagavad Gita* every day. My connection to the supreme power grew stronger. I felt safe. I felt protected.

Ten months after treatment, a thought began to take root — I needed to go to Canada. I needed closure. I needed to be where my mother had spent her final days. My visa, which had arrived just four days after she passed, was valid until February 2025. The summer of 2024 would be my only chance to go before winter set in.

I began planning the trip with a friend to Amsterdam and from there on to Canada. For two months we kept planning. But somehow, the plans kept falling through. At one point, I told myself, *It's okay, just cancel. Mom isn't there anymore.*

That night — or rather, early morning — I had a dream.

In it, the phone rang. I picked it up.

It was my mother. Her voice was clear, warm, exactly as I remembered. She questioned me in Marathi, "Why are you not coming? I'm here."

Shocked, I ask her, "Mom, is that really you?"

She answers, "Yes, it's really me."

My heart felt it was going to burst with the intense pain I experienced.

Crying bitterly, I ask, "Mom, you're there? But everyone is saying you're not there anymore!"

She kept reassuring me, over and over, "I'm here… come here."

When I woke, my chest ached. It was heavy, as though I had truly cried in my sleep.

Was it just a dream? Or was it a call from beyond?

Who can ever say? The living call it a dream. The heart calls it a meeting.

CHAPTER 33

2024, CANADA — WHEN LOVE REACHES ACROSS WORLDS

It so happened that a school friend came to Pune to attend a wedding with her husband from Bangalore. I invited them to stay over for a couple of days after the wedding.

That evening, as we sat chatting, she asked about my trip to Amsterdam and Canada. I told her it had fizzled out. Her husband turned to her and said, "Why don't you go with her?" And just like that — within an hour — the plan was finalised.

He even booked our hotels in Amsterdam right there and then. I had been planning for two months and nothing had happened, but here it was decided in two hours. It felt as if some unknown force was making sure I could finally get my closure.

That April, I set out to see the tulip fields… and to visit my brother in Canada.

In Canada, I was put up in my mother's room. Everything had been cleared out, except for her walking stick. The first time I lay down on her bed, it felt like I was floating on clouds — soft, warm, and comforting. It was the strangest feeling, as if something invisible to the eye but very real was holding me.

I slept peacefully, wrapped in a sense of safety I couldn't explain. Many times during my stay, I felt a presence — loving, gentle, reassuring.

My brother and sister-in-law took me to all the places connected with my mother's last days — the hospital, the spot where her last rites were performed, and the place where her ashes were scattered. It gave me a kind of closure.

One afternoon, while lying awake on the bed, I felt a light touch on my hand — a slow caress. I was looking at my hand even as I felt it. It felt like fingers were caressing my hand lovingly, except there was no one there. A sudden wave of fear passed through me — and after that, the presence never returned… or perhaps it simply never let me feel it again. That, I shall never know.

Some meetings happen in dreams. Some happen in the quiet, when love reaches across worlds to touch your hand. But many a times, our inability to understand — and to accept without fear that there are dimensions beyond the one we live in — becomes the very barrier to that communication.

When I was in India, it was easy to pretend that Mom was maybe alive somewhere in Canada. But now, there was no denying the truth — she was gone. Forever.

Wherever she is, I know she loves me and watches over me. And I hope she has forgiven me for hiding my brain malignancy diagnosis from her. She left this world completely oblivious to that truth.

Love you, Mom. You are not just a piece of my heart… you are a piece of my soul.

CHAPTER 34

2025, PUNE — HELD BY GRACE

Back home, I was more at peace with all that had happened — my not being able to see Mom before she passed, my illness, everything.

All that mattered now was the ability to live in the present moment. I felt happier and complete in myself.

I know no one has gotten out of this world alive. Someday, we all must take that final journey. But now I know — I am not alone. My Guruji will carry me through whatever is written in my destiny. I have nothing to fear.

My brain MRI continues for now. What the future holds and when is something I have left to the Supreme Power. It is up to Him to decide how much suffering I may or may not have to go through.

I continue to live life to the fullest. Grateful for each sunrise. I travel because it is my passion. I live my dreams. I participated in a music video. I always wanted to record a song — and a very gracious music teacher in Mumbai helped me realise that dream. I will always be grateful to her for guiding me and making me a part of the music video. I now enjoy the company of family and friends more than ever before. Each moment holds more value now.

I had this strong need to do something positive — to help others going through a challenging health journey. At first, I thought I could talk to patients in support groups. Then I realised I could reach more people through today's social media platforms.

Social media handles can be a bit challenging for people of my day and age. We have seen technology grow from black-and-white photographs to coloured ones. Single channel on TV to multiple channels on OTT and from booking trunk calls to making WhatsApp calls anywhere in the world. But nothing can stop a determined mind.

I started an Instagram account (**cancerwar1**) and began sharing my experiences and what helped me. Then came the thought of sharing other people's inspirational journeys on YouTube, I started my YouTube channel (**warriorvoiceswithsangita**).

This book is also a small contribution to the world — a reminder that, however difficult our life journey may be, we have the power to choose how we face it.

What is the point of worrying about what may happen tomorrow? I have left all my worries at the feet of my Guru. He will decide what's good for me.

I live in the present moment.

I choose faith.

Faith in my Guru.

Faith in God.

Faith in myself.

Faith in miracles.

And so, I walk on — not knowing where the road bends, but trusting that each step is lit by a light far greater than my own.

Some days the sky will be clear, some days it may rain, yet in every season, I carry the quiet knowing that I am held.

In that knowing, there is no fear, only gratitude for the gift of this breath, this moment, this life.

Love and blessings from me to all of you.

Jai Gurudev 🙏